WORLD: Kayaking and Canoeing

Paul Mason

A&C Black • London

Produced for A & C Black by
Monkey Puzzle Media Ltd
48 York Avenue
Hove BN3 1PJ, UK

Published by A & C Black
Bloomsbury Publishing Plc
49 - 51 Bedford Square
London
W1CB 3DP

Published 2011
First published in hardback 2010
Copyright © 2010 A & C Black

ISBN 978-1-4081-3049-0

A CIP catalogue record for this book is
available from the British Library.

Editor: Dan Rogers
Design: Mayer Media Ltd
Picture research: Lynda Lines

This book is produced using paper that
is made from wood grown in managed,
sustainable forests. It is natural,
renewable and recyclable. The logging
and manufacturing processes conform
to the environmental regulations of the
country of origin.

Printed and bound in China by
C&C Offset Printing Co.,Ltd

Picture acknowledgements
Dawn Adams p. 13; Alamy pp. 7 (Joe
Fox), 11 top (Ashley Cooper); Aurora-
Pathfinders p. 14; Canoe Kayak and
Paddle Co p. 17; Cardeli Photography
p. 19; Carol Kane Photography p. 22
(photographersdirect.com); Corbis
p. 20 (John G. Mabanglo/epa); Getty
Images pp. 1 (Karl Weatherly), 8 (Jeff
Foott), 9 (Jupiterimages), 21, 25 top
(Karl Weatherly), 25 bottom (Jock
Montgomery), 27 (Skip Brown); Tim
Harvey p. 18; JoPe Fors & Fjäll p. 15
(Jonas Persson); Laurence Delderfield
Photography p. 6 (photographersdirect.
com); MPM Images pp. 26, 28; Nature
Picture Library p. 5 (Jerry Monkman);
Photolibrary pp. 4 (Monkey Business
Images), 16 (Douglas Peebles), 23 (Simon
Albertini-LOOK-foto), 29 (Mike Tittel);
Wikimedia Commons pp. 10, 11 bottom;
Yukon River Quest p. 12–13 (Jeff Brady).
Compass rose artwork on front cover
and inside pages by iStockphoto. Map
artwork by MPM Images.

The front cover shows a kayaker in the
falls on the Wind River, North Cascade
Range, USA (Corbis/Richard Hallman/
Aurora Photos).

Every effort has been made to
contact copyright holders of material
reproduced in this book. Any omissions
will be rectified in subsequent printings
if notice is given to the publishers.

SAFETY ADVICE

Don't attempt any of the
activities or techniques
in this book without the
guidance of a qualified
instructor.

CONTENTS

Paddling Dreamland

As you paddle along the river, the roaring noise ahead gets louder. Next, you see smoky spray floating in the air. Your stomach knots with excitement – it's too late to turn back now. The river drops steeply down, churning and boiling. The boat becomes a wild horse, bucking and twisting. This is the world of kayaking and canoeing!

THE SECRET LANGUAGE OF PADDLING

paddling kayaking or canoeing
coaming outwards-curving lip of a kayak's cockpit
day hatch opening to a small storage area inside a kayak

DREAM TICKET

Imagine you could go **paddling** anywhere in the world – would you know where to go? Where are the best kayaking and canoeing spots for beginners, improvers and experts? This book can help you decide the places that should be on your list.

Kayaking down a chute of white water. Kayaking and canoeing can take you to places you would otherwise never see.

Technical: Kayaking and canoeing

Kayaking is done using a long paddle with a blade on each end. Canoeing is done with a shorter paddle, which has a blade only on one end. Each can be done on almost any kind of water, and in many different kinds of boat:

Sea and river touring:

• Touring boats are longer than white-water boats and have space for luggage and supplies.

• They are stable and hard to tip over but not as manoeuvrable.

• The boats are often fitted with rudders to make them easier to steer.

White-water kayaking:

• White-water boats tend to be shorter and wider than touring boats, with flatter bottoms.

• They tip over more easily but are much more manoeuvrable.

• White-water boats are used in rivers and in ocean surf.

Open boats:

• Open boats are often called Canadian canoes.

• They can fit several people and are great for fishing and for camping trips.

• Some people also use open boats in white water.

Even open-topped Canadian canoes such as this one can be taken into white water by expert paddlers.

Hints and tips

Of course, when you begin your dream trip, you'll need to be sure you know what you're doing. You'll need to know your **coaming** from your **day hatch,** for example. So we also tell you some key paddling words, what each location is like, the kind of equipment you'll need, tips from local paddlers, and advice on technique. In fact, this book is your passport to the world of canoeing and kayaking.

Gorge d'Ardèche

The Ardèche region of France is in the warm, sunny south of the country. The mountains here are made of limestone. Over the centuries rivers have carved steep-sided valleys, or gorges, through them. One of the most popular gorges for canoeing and kayaking is the one carved by the River Ardèche.

GORGE D'ARDÈCHE
Location: south-eastern France
Type of paddling: touring
Difficulty level: 1 of 5
Best season: May to September

WHY THE GORGE D'ARDÈCHE?

This is a great place to have your first try at an overnight **touring** trip, paddling in the day and camping beside the river at night. There are two official camping grounds along the gorge. The river itself does not flow so fast or steeply that the paddling is difficult. Even so, there are short sections of rougher water to keep things interesting.

A group of kayakers begin their journey down the Gorge d'Ardèche. The arch in the background is the Pont-d'Arc.

Launching a kayak

There are two main ways to launch a kayak: from a beach and from a jetty. To launch from a beach, people sit their boat in very shallow water, climb in, and thrust it forwards using their hips. From a jetty, it's a bit more complicated:

PADDLING THE GORGE D'ARDÈCHE

Most people start near the Pont-d'Arc, a 60-metre (197-foot) high arch of across the river. Ahead are 30 kilometres (18.6 miles) of paddling, and a night or two of sleeping beside the river. Along the way are 30-metre (98-foot) cliffs, pebbly beaches, and rock shelves that make great picnic spots. You finally haul the boat from the water at the other end of the gorge, at the ancient town of St-Martin d'Ardèche.

1. With the boat next to the jetty, lay the paddle across behind the **cockpit**, with one end still on the jetty.

2. Climb in, holding the paddle shaft against the rear edge of cockpit to keep the boat steady.

3. Once you are sitting down, lift the paddle over your head so it's in front of you.

4. Fasten the **spray skirt** and paddle away.

Launching a kayak from an ocean beach: once your boat is afloat, paddle straight at any waves and punch through them

THE SECRET LANGUAGE OF PADDLING

touring taking a long trip that involves an overnight stay

cockpit hole in the deck of a kayak where the paddler sits

spray skirt cover for the cockpit, designed to stop water getting in

San Juan Archipelago

SAN JUAN ARCHIPELAGO
Location: USA/Canada
Type of paddling: **sea kayaking**, touring
Difficulty level: 2 of 5
Best season: June to September

If you were trying to imagine a perfect place for exploring in a sea kayak or Canadian canoe, you couldn't think of anywhere better than the San Juan **Archipelago**. The islands in the archipelago are split between the USA and Canada. The US side is the San Juan Islands, and the Canadian side is the Gulf Islands.

WHY THE SAN JUAN ARCHIPELAGO?

In the deep channels between the islands swim sea lions and killer whales. (One of the islands is even called Orcas Island – orca is the old name for killer whales.) On the islands themselves there are bears, and you have a good chance of seeing a bald eagle floating through the skies above your boat.

THE SECRET LANGUAGE OF PADDLING

sea kayaking kayaking on the ocean, usually as a way of exploring the coastline and nearby islands

archipelago group of islands

There can't be many places where paddlers can share a stretch of water with killer whales.

Technical: Kit

On a warm day, in warm water, you do not need any special equipment to give kayaking or canoeing a quick try. Once you get more into the sport, though, proper kit is important – especially if the weather or water is cold, or you are out on the water for over an hour.

• Helmet
Protects head if paddler is tipped from boat

• Wetsuit top (for cold) or **waterproof top** (for warmer weather)
Tight cuffs stop water from running up your sleeves
Keeps the sun off your skin, preventing burning

• Flotation vest
Helps paddler stay afloat if he or she is tipped from the boat

• Spray skirt
Attaches to coaming and stops water getting into cockpit

• Wetsuit bottoms (for cold) or **shorts** (in warmer conditions)

• Boots
Make walking on pebbly or rocky beaches and river bottoms safer and more comfortable

Tip from a Local

It's great fun to go paddling with a group of friends at sunset – people come from far away to see the beautiful sunsets over the archipelago.

PADDLING THE SAN JUAN ARCHIPELAGO
The archipelago has something for everyone. In total there are over 150 islands, many of them only a short distance apart. Most are uninhabited, so the wildlife is able to roam freely. The archipelago is sheltered from the Pacific Ocean by Vancouver Island, which is much larger, so the sea is normally calm enough for paddling.

If you like the San Juan Archipelago...

... you could also try:
• the Outer Banks lagoons, USA
• Tasmania, Australia
They're great for exploring by boat.

River Dunajec

Slovakia is a small country, but it's big in the world of kayaking and canoeing. This is home to Michal Martikán, winner of two Olympic and seven World Championship gold medals for **white-water** canoeing. Fortunately, you don't have to be as good as Martikán to canoe here. For less-experienced paddlers, the River Dunajec is a great place to start.

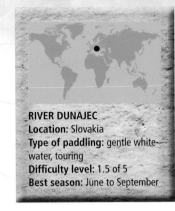

RIVER DUNAJEC
Location: Slovakia
Type of paddling: gentle white-water, touring
Difficulty level: 1.5 of 5
Best season: June to September

Tip from a Local

If you fancy a change one day, try climbing Trzy Korony, the Three Crowns mountain – the viewing platform at the top of the highest peak has incredible views of the river.

THE SECRET LANGUAGE OF PADDLING

white water rough, bumpy sections of river or, in the sea, breaking waves

deck top of a kayak

rafting using a raft – a flat, wide boat that you sit on

WHY RIVER DUNAJEC?

The River Dunajec has paddling to suit most people. Some stretches are calm and slow flowing, with fantastic views of the local countryside. In the distance looms a mountain named Trzy Korony, which means "three crowns". You might even spot one of the traditional wooden rafts, called *plt'*, piloted by guides dressed in the local costume.

Setting off down the steep-sided gorge of the Dunajec.

SKILL

Wet exit

One thing is almost certain about kayaking – at some point, the boat will tip over with you in it. If you are paddling a boat with a cockpit and spray skirt, a technique called a "wet exit" will get you out safely.

1. The boat tips over, trapping the paddler underneath.

2. The paddler pulls the front of spray skirt loose, using the pull tag. (It's very important that the tag doesn't accidentally get tucked under the

Once you are out of the kayak, keep hold of it (it will help if you try to come up facing it, instead of wondering where it is like this paddler!).

coaming when the skirt is put on, or it will be impossible to reach in an emergency.)

3. Once the skirt is off, the paddler rolls forwards, with his or her head going towards the **deck** of the boat.

4. Finally, the paddler pushes out of the cockpit.

PADDLING THE RIVER DUNAJEC

The highlight of the river is a 10-kilometre (6.2-mile) long gorge called Prielom Dunajca, or Dunajec Canyon. The river picks up speed here, and in places there are white-water sections. Paddlers and **rafters** zip quickly past the steep cliffs. This area is a nature reserve, and there's always the chance that you will surprise an otter or two – or maybe even a lynx, the area's biggest predator.

A traditional plt' raft heads down the Dunajec, with the Three Crowns mountain in the background.

If you like the River Dunajec...

... you could also try:
• Murray River, Australia
• Moisie River, Quebec, Canada
• Ozark National Scenic Riverways, USA
They are all good for canoe and kayak touring.

Yukon River Quest

The Yukon River Quest is definitely designed for the kind of person who likes a challenge. The event advertises itself as the longest kayak and canoe race in the world. The competitors travel an amazing 740 kilometres (460 miles), following the Yukon River north from Whitehorse to Dawson City.

YUKON RIVER QUEST
Location: Yukon River, Canada
Type of paddling: long-distance
Difficulty level: 5 of 5
Time of year: June and July

WILDERNESS RACING

The race passes through the Canadian wilderness. The official introduction says: "Teams should anticipate that they may spend many hours at a time out of sight of any other boat or living person. The Yukon River has very few road access points, and very few people live along its banks." In other words, if you get into trouble, you have to be able to get yourself out of it.

Tip from a Local
Your biggest enemy is the cold – make sure you have plenty of warm, dry clothes if you want to finish the race.

A big team in a voyageur canoe hits a rough patch, in a (relatively) narrow section of river.

RACE FORMAT

The race is open to tandem canoeists and kayakers, teams paddling large open canoes (called **voyageur** canoes), and solo paddlers in any of the three kinds of boat. There are also prizes for men, women and mixed teams.

THE SECRET LANGUAGE OF PADDLING

voyageur another name for Canadian canoes, which comes from old-time Canadian wilderness travellers called *voyageurs*

LONG DAYS, SHORT NIGHTS

This far north, the nights are very short during summertime. The sun rises at 4.30 in the morning, and sets at 11.30 at night. The racers have about 19 hours of daylight in which to paddle. The fastest-ever finishing time was set in 2008, when a team of six in a voyageur canoe finished in 39 hours, 32 minutes and 43 seconds.

If you like the Yukon River Quest...

... you could also try:
- the Queen Lili'uokalani Canoe Race, Hawaii
- the Devizes to Westminster International Canoe Race, England

Both are long-distance challenges.

The start of the Yukon River Quest. These paddlers will have sore hands by the time they reach the finish, 740 kilometres (460 miles) later.

River Teith

One thing you definitely need for kayaking is water. And if there's one thing Scotland has plenty of, it's water. It rains a LOT here. That might be bad if you like holidays featuring a lot of lying by the pool sipping a cold drink – but if you're a paddler, it's good news.

RIVER TEITH
Location: Scotland
Type of paddling: gentle white-water
Difficulty level: 2 of 5
Best season: May to September

If you like the River Teith...

... you could also try:
• River Barle, England
• South Fork of the American River, USA
Both have sections that are good for a first attempt at white-water paddling.

Shooting a section of white water on the Teith, in a Canadian canoe.

WHY THE RIVER TEITH?

The River Teith is popular because it is an ideal river for beginners to try white-water paddling. There are white-water sections along a good stretch of the river, which give plenty of chances for thrills. But there is only one section that is tricky for beginners, so there are unlikely to be any spills.

Tip from a Local

If you want to do something different one day, the nearby Trossach mountains are a great place for some mountain walking.

Paddling the River Teith

The most popular section of the Teith runs from Callander to Stirling Bridge, a 23-kilometre (14-mile) paddle. After a gentle start, the river hits the Torrie **Rapid**, where things start to get interesting. Soon afterwards there are two small **drops** to deal with. About halfway down, some paddlers **portage** their boats rather than try to make it down Deanston Weir. Below the weir the river widens and there are several islands.

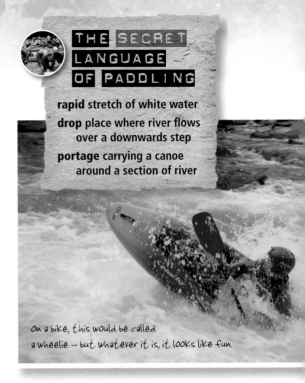

THE SECRET LANGUAGE OF PADDLING

rapid stretch of white water

drop place where river flows over a downwards step

portage carrying a canoe around a section of river

On a bike, this would be called a wheelie – but whatever it is, it looks like fun.

Technical: White-water grades

White-water sections of rivers are given grades, which show how dangerous they are to paddle down.

Grade 1
Easy to paddle, but may have some small waves.

Grade 2
Slightly larger waves, plus other obstacles to avoid.

Grade 3
Larger obstacles again, and the paddler will have to follow a particular route to make it safely through.

Grade 4
Big obstacles and without an obvious way down. Often needs to be looked at from the bank before paddling.

Grade 5
Extremely difficult, experts-only rapids. Looking before you paddle is essential.

Grade 6
Most people would think a Grade 6 river cannot be paddled. Those who try have a good chance of going to hospital.

Grades are only an indication: a river that is dangerous when a lot of water flows down it, for example, might be less dangerous with only a little water.

Salmon River, Middle Fork

Idaho is sometimes known as the "potato state" because so many potatoes are grown there. Few people also know that Idaho has more official wilderness areas than any other US state, apart from Alaska. One of the best ways to see these wildernesses is by paddling down a river such as the Salmon River.

As well as kayakers and canoeists, white-water rafters are allowed a few slots on the Middle Fork of the Salmon River each year.

SALMON RIVER, MIDDLE FORK
Location: Idaho, USA
Type of paddling: white-water, touring
Difficulty level: 3 of 5
Best season: June to September

WHY MIDDLE FORK?

A trip down the Middle **Fork** of the Salmon River is a real wilderness experience. Each night for a week or so you camp beside the river. There are great rapids, beautiful countryside, and the chance to see all kinds of wildlife. There are bears, wolves, and cougars in the woods – something to remember at night when you're camping beside the river.

Paddling Middle Fork

You need a permit to paddle the Middle Fork, and permits are hard to get. If you do get one, you aren't allowed to leave anything – not even your poo – behind in the wilderness. So why do people come? It's because few of the rapids are harder than Grade 3. They're exciting, and sometimes scary, but improvers as well as experts can ride them.

If you like the Salmon River...

... you could also try:
• River Taff, Wales
• Yarra River, Australia
• Nahanni River, Canada
They are also good for kayak touring.

Tip from a Local

Only limited numbers are allowed on the Salmon River's Middle Fork – for the chance of a slot, you have to put your name into a lottery.

THE SECRET LANGUAGE OF PADDLING

fork one of two or more channels of a river

SKILL
River hazards

To paddle safely down rapids, you need to be able to "read the river". This means being able to look at how the water moves, then work out what lies under the surface. Only then can you decide a safe way through.

This kayaker has read the river right, and has safely paddled through a section of white water.

These are some common features of white water:

• Water in bumps or small, irregular waves – this happens where the river is shallow.

• Standing waves – these happen where the river suddenly gets deeper, or where a narrow channel widens.

• Stoppers – also called keepers, these backwards-flowing waves can be strong enough to trap a kayak in their grip.

• Chutes – channels of calm, fast-flowing water that show where the river is deeper. These can provide a safe way through rapids.

Santa Cruz

Most paddlers get their thrills on rivers, especially the ones who enjoy a bumpy ride on the white water. But those who live near – or visit – the ocean have another way of getting their kicks. They go **surf paddling**, riding the ocean swell like surfers. Surf paddlers either use boats similar to white-water ones, or sit-on-top wave skis.

SANTA CRUZ
Location: Portugal
Type of paddling: surf paddling
Difficulty level: 3 of 5
Best season: June to October for warmth, September to June for waves

Why Santa Cruz?

Santa Cruz is a great place to try surf kayaking. Portugal has excellent waves, good weather, and is a beautiful place to visit. It's one of the surfing world's best-kept secrets, and the uncrowded beaches make it a good place to practise in the waves.

"I know! Just in case the judges don't spot my amazing aerials, I'll paddle a bright pink boat as well." Result.

If you like Santa Cruz...

... you could also try:
• Saunton Sands, England
• Santa Cruz, California, USA
Both are good for surf paddling.

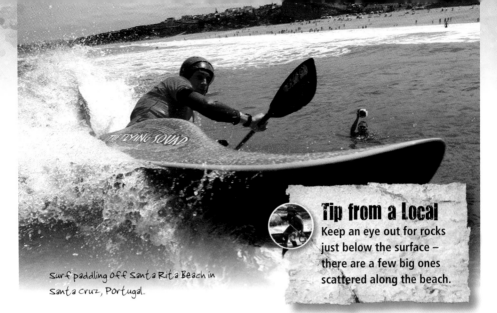

Surf paddling off Santa Rita Beach in Santa Cruz, Portugal.

Tip from a Local
Keep an eye out for rocks just below the surface – there are a few big ones scattered along the beach.

PADDLING SANTA CRUZ

First of all, make sure that the waves aren't too big. Portugal gets surf over 4 metres (13 feet) high, which would be dangerous even for the greatest experts. The best-sized wave to practise on is about 1 metre (3.3 feet) high. There is usually a time gap between each **set** of waves, and it's best to wait for a gap before paddling out as fast as you can. Once you're **out the back**, you can pick a nice-looking wave to ride back to the beach.

THE SECRET LANGUAGE OF PADDLING

surf paddling kayaking or canoeing on the ocean, paddling out before riding back in on the waves

set group of waves that arrive at the beach one after another

out the back past the area where waves start to break

SKILL
Surf etiquette

Waves can be very powerful, and they are especially dangerous when crowded. Surfers have developed a set of rules so that people can share the waves safely and fairly:

• If you are riding a wave, it is your job to avoid other people, not their job to get out of the way.

• You must always be in control of your kayak/wave ski/surfboard. If you're NOT in control, go back in to the beach.

• The first person to catch a wave has the right to ride it. Don't try to join him or her – this is called "dropping in", and is NEVER welcome.

• If two people catch a wave at the same time, the one closest to where it broke has the right to ride it.

19

The Olympics

Most kayakers and canoeists take part in the sport for fun. They enjoy the challenge of getting down a particular river, or they like the peace and quiet of touring or sea kayaking. But there's a hard core of professional paddlers who take part in competitions. For them, the biggest dream is that they will one day take part in – or even win – the Olympic Games.

THE OLYMPICS
Location: various
Type of paddling: racing, white-water
Difficulty level: 5 of 5
Held: every four years

Jennifer Bongardt of Germany powers through a downstream gate close to the end of the course at the 2008 Beijing Olympic Games.

SPRINT CANOEING AND KAYAKING

One of the Olympic contests is called the sprint. This is a speed-based race in a straight line, a bit like the 100 metres on the athletics track. The races last either 500 metres or 1000 metres (1640 or 3280 feet), and there are events for both kayaking and canoeing. The contests work on a knockout format, with the top paddlers in each **round** going through to the next round until there is a winner.

THE SECRET LANGUAGE OF PADDLING

round race that forms one part of a bigger competition

gate pair of poles hanging down, through which the paddler has to pass

Sprint canoeists race away from the start of a race at the Beijing Olympics in 2008.

SLALOM CANOEING AND KAYAKING

Slalom races are held on white-water courses. In modern Olympics the courses are artificial, so that the water flow can be controlled and is the same for each racer. The competitors have to manoeuvre through a series of **gates**, sometimes paddling downstream and sometimes upstream. If they touch a gate, a two-second penalty is added to their overall time. Like the sprint races, slalom follows a knockout format.

Summer Isles

Sea paddling is a great way to explore a small group of islands such as the Summer Isles. You see wildlife and scenery that would be impossible to view in almost any other way. And when you're hungry you can just pull your boat up on to a beautiful beach, unpack your sandwiches, and tuck in.

SUMMER ISLES
Location: Scotland
Type of paddling: sea paddling
Difficulty level: 3 of 5
Best season: May to September

Kayaking in the Summer Isles. Set out a fishing line or two, catch your lunch, and then paddle ashore to cook it on the beach.

WHY THE SUMMER ISLES?

The Summer Isles, off Scotland's west coast, are a sea paddler's paradise. They have relatively sheltered seas and beautiful coastlines. The wildlife is amazing, on land, in the air, and in the ocean. If you like the idea of paddling along with dolphins or seals popping up next to the boat, this is the place to come.

PADDLING THE SUMMER ISLES

Most people start their trip from the mainland. It is a 3-kilometre (1.9-mile) paddle to get to Tanera Mor, the largest island (and the only one where people live). Next they can pick where to head for:
• The beautiful sandstone cliffs of Mol Mor
• The natural stone arch on Tanera Beg
• The seals and other wildlife on the tiny islands to the north-east.
On the way back to the mainland, the views of the Scottish Highlands will take your breath away (if the paddling hasn't already).

Technical: Picking a campsite

One of the great things about exploring in a kayak is that you can get to islands and beaches that almost no one else can reach. Sometimes you can even camp on them.

It's important that your campsite is safe, whether you're camping on a river beach or beside the ocean:

• Make sure you are sleeping above the highest level the water can reach. Most beaches have a line of sticks, plants and other debris that has washed up at this high-water point.

• Pull your boat up out of the water and tie it up securely. Most people use two ropes, in case one breaks. The ropes should have enough slack to let the boat float if the water level rises.

A perfect campsite for the night, beside the Isar River in Germany.

If you like the Summer Isles...

... you could also try:
• Vancouver Island, Canada
• The Uists and Benbecula, Scotland
They're also good for exploring by sea.

Tip from a Local

Check the wind direction before you set off – paddling back to the mainland with the wind in your face is very tiring.

Rio Futaleufú

The Patagonia region of South America is a white-water paddler's delight. Patagonia is beside the Andes Mountains. In summer, the snow and ice high in the Andes melt, and the **meltwater** rushes down through Patagonia's steep river valleys. The clear mountain water gives many rivers – Rio Futaleufú among them – a beautiful, bright-blue colour.

RIO FUTALEUFÚ
Location: Chile
Type of paddling: white-water
Difficulty level: 4 of 5
Best season: December to April

WHY RIO FUTALEUFÚ?

This is one of the best white-water rivers in Patagonia, or indeed the world. It is wider and faster flowing than almost any other river. The combination of rapids at various grades, bright-blue water, isolation (the river is far from any city or town), and beautiful surroundings make this a must-visit river for any expert kayaker.

If you like Rio Futaleufú...

… you could also try:
• River Karnali, Nepal
• River Chatkal, Uzbekistan and Kyrgyzstan
They are also very isolated.

PADDLING

There are some sections of the river that are Grade 2, but the Rio Futaleufú is mainly Grade 3 to 5. The names of the rapids give some idea of what to expect: Terminator, or Inferno Canyon, for example. This is a river where it's a good idea to paddle with a local guide. They know the danger points, and where to find the portages for impossible sections of the river.

THE SECRET LANGUAGE OF PADDLING

meltwater water from melted snow or ice
paddle shaft tube with paddle blade or blades on the end

Tip from a Local

If you get tired of paddling one day, take a walk up to Las Tres Monjas – the three volcanic peaks whose name means "the three nuns".

At full flow, Rio Futaleufú poses a challenge even to the best kayakers in the world.

SKILL
Eskimo roll

In white-water kayaking, one of the most important techniques is the Eskimo roll. This is a method of flipping your kayak back upright after it has tipped over, without having to get out and drag it to the bank.

1. The kayak goes over. Immediately lean forwards and twist round, to get your paddle to the surface of the water and parallel with the side of the boat. Keep both hands on the **paddle shaft**.

2. Turn the paddle sideways to the boat, with the blade flat on the surface.

3. Pull yourself up on the paddle, and at the same time snap your hip quickly upwards, toward the surface. It is the

Lever on the paddle, and snap your hips up at the surface, and you should pop out of the water like this. Get this perfect in calm, safe water before trying it anywhere else.

hip movement that brings you up, NOT the pull against the paddle.

4. You should emerge from the water with the boat twisting upright at the same time.

Colorado River

The Colorado River snakes its way through western USA. It passes beautiful rock formations, Indian ruins, amazing wildlife, and – most breathtaking of all – the Grand Canyon. The river carved this giant canyon, which is over 1.8 kilometres (1.1 miles) deep, and so big it can be seen from space.

COLORADO RIVER
Location: Arizona, USA
Type of paddling: white-water
Difficulty level: 3.5 of 5
Best season: April to October

WHY THE COLORADO RIVER?

Of course, for a paddler the big canyon, the wonderful scenery and wildlife alone aren't enough. Kayakers and canoeists want white water, too! Fortunately the Colorado has plenty of that: some rapids are Grade 5, and for experts only. But many of the others are Grades 2, 3 or 4, and can be paddled by improvers (especially if they are with a guide).

Tip from a Local

If you want a permit to paddle down the Grand Canyon, you'd better be patient – there's currently a 12-year waiting list.

The Colorado River isn't this calm all the way down! A lone kayaker sets off on a trip through the Grand Canyon.

Paddling the Colorado River

The Colorado is one of the longest rivers in the USA. Kayaking trips can last anything from hours to weeks. One of the toughest rapids in the area must be the 11 kilometres (6.8 miles) of Rock Creek (a **tributary** of the Colorado), which are graded 5+. The Grand Canyon itself is graded 4+. You have to get a permit to paddle without a guide in the Grand Canyon. The only other way to get on the river is by paying to be part of an organized group.

THE SECRET LANGUAGE OF PADDLING

tributary river that feeds into another

If you like the Colorado River...

... you could also try:
- River Kinglas, Scotland, for radical white water
- River Danube, Europe, for long-distance trips

Using guidebooks

Many white-water rivers are described in guidebooks for paddlers. Big rivers such as the Colorado even get whole books about only that one river. This is the type of information guidebooks contain:

- Distances from place to place, and white-water grade of any rapids.

- Put-in points: these are where routes start, the places where it's possible to put your kayak in the water.

- Water level: the ideal height of water in the river. Most guidebooks give a way of working out the water level, for example: "If the stone slabs beside the bridge are covered, the water is high enough. If it reaches the banks, the level is too high."

- Description: a step-by-step description of any rapids, including advice about how to get through them and any potential hazards.

- Take-out points: places where you can take your boat out of the water to finish the route or in case something goes wrong.

oops! using a guidebook allows you to work out possible danger spots – and hopefully to avoid them

27

Tongariro River

New Zealand is a wonderful place to visit if you're a paddler. The two main islands, called North and South Island, have jagged coastlines with inlets, rivers and rocky headlands to explore from the sea. Inland, the steep, high mountains combine with lots of rain to make some of the best white-water rivers in the world.

WHY THE TONGARIRO RIVER?

The Tongariro River flows steeply down through a volcanic plateau, which lies at the heart of New Zealand's North Island. The river finally empties into Lake Taupo, but before then it crashes and rumbles its way through 60 Grade 3 and 4 rapids. The river is a favourite with people paddling both kayaks and **rafts**.

TONGARIRO RIVER
Location: North Island, New Zealand
Type of paddling: white-water
Difficulty level: 4 of 5
Best season: all year round, after heavy rain

If you like the Tongariro River...

... you could also try:
• River Tavy, England
• Padas River, Malaysia
They also offer Grade 3 and 4 paddling.

"Again! Again!" Happy rafters reach the end of a run down the Tongariro River.

PADDLING THE TONGARIRO RIVER

The most popular part of the Tongariro is a section that includes all 60 Grade 3 and 4 rapids. The boats go into the river at the Poutu water intake on the Waikato Falls Road. Three hours later, they are taken out at the Red Hut Pool. You need to be fit for this one – it's a lung-busting paddle along some of the fastest-flowing water in New Zealand.

THE SECRET LANGUAGE OF PADDLING

raft tough inflatable boat that can be paddled down white-water rivers

Tip from a Local

If you visit the Tongariro, make sure you give the fishing a try – this is one of the world's best trout-fishing rivers.

You probably would need a rest in a quiet eddy after tackling a waterfall like this one (above).

Technical: White-water safety

White-water paddling can be extremely dangerous. This basic set of guidelines helps make it as safe as possible:

• You are responsible for your own safety. If something makes you uncomfortable, or you doubt that you can do it, don't try. Never be bullied or persuaded by someone else.

• Be a confident swimmer. If you are not, white-water paddling is not for you.

• Never go white-water paddling alone.

• Do not paddle in the dark. Make sure you have plenty of time to finish any paddle in daylight.

• Always, ALWAYS wear a floatation vest, a helmet, and the right kind of clothing.

Glossary

Words from the Secret Language features

archipelago group of islands

coaming outwards-curving lip of a kayak's cockpit

cockpit hole in the deck of a kayak where the paddler sits

day hatch opening to a small storage area inside a kayak

deck top of a kayak

drop place where river flows over a downwards step

fork one of two or more channels of a river

gate pair of poles hanging down, through which the paddler has to pass

meltwater water from melted snow or ice

out the back past the area where waves start to break

paddle shaft tube with paddle blade or blades on the end

paddling kayaking or canoeing

portage carrying a canoe around a section of river

raft tough inflatable boat that can be paddled down white-water rivers

rafting using a raft – a flat, wide boat that you sit on

rapid stretch of white water

round race that forms one part of a bigger competition

sea kayaking kayaking on the ocean, usually as a way of exploring the coastline and nearby islands

set group of waves that arrive at the beach one after another

spray skirt cover for the cockpit, designed to stop water getting in

surf paddling kayaking or canoeing on the ocean, paddling out before riding back in on the waves

touring taking a long trip that involves an overnight stay

tributary river that feeds into another

voyageur another name for Canadian canoes, which comes from old-time Canadian wilderness travellers called *voyageurs*

white water rough, bumpy sections of river or, in the sea, breaking waves

Other words paddlers use

access point place on the bank of the river where you can put in or take out a boat

backpaddle paddle backwards to slow, stop or reverse the boat's movement

bladder air sac inside a boat, designed to stop it sinking even if the boat tips over

bow front end of a boat

eddy calm area of water, away from the main current

flat water water with little or no movement or disturbances on it

folding canoe canoe that can be folded up and carried, for example in the rear of a car

grab loop loop or handle on the bow or stern of a kayak, which allows it to be towed or carried

stern the back end of a boat

Finding Out More

The Internet

www.ukriversguidebook.co.uk/rivers.htm
This is a great resource for UK paddlers, dividing the country into different areas, then listing rivers that are good for touring, easy white water, intermediate/advanced white water, and extreme white water.

www.ukseakayakguidebook.co.uk
A sister site to ukriversguidebook, this has reports on over 100 sea trips by kayak, in England, Scotland, Wales and Ireland.

www.seapaddler.co.uk
Although UK-based, this is an excellent site for sea kayakers everywhere, with coaching advice, information about travel destinations around the world, hints and tips, advice on equipment, and lots more.

Magazines

Canoe and Kayak
This is the UK's biggest paddling magazine. It carries articles about technique, equipment reviews, interviews with top-level paddlers, and news about contests and the canoe and kayak industry. The magazine also has a website at **www.canoekayak.co.uk.**

Paddler
One of the leading canoe and kayak magazines in the USA. It includes equipment tests, interviews, and other news, and takes a wider-ranging view than some other magazines, with articles from North America, Europe and the rest of the world. The magazine's website is at **www.paddlermagazine.com.**

Books

Canoeing and Kayaking Yvonne Thorpe (Franklin Watts, 2009)

Canoeing and Kayaking Lois Rock (Wayland, 2009)

Kayaking and Rafting Paul Mason (Macmillan Library, 2007)

Each of these children's books introduces the basic skills and techniques of kayaking and canoeing for beginners, and gives advice about equipment and clothing. The third book also has information about white-water rafting.

Index